Magnet Man
and Me

Written by Lindsay Galvin

Illustrated by Alex Lopez

Collins

Boom! A bright flash of sparks. A red-hot thing shimmers, melting the road!

Dad is asleep, snoring. I tap his arm.
"What is it, Brook?" he says.

The red-hot thing turns silver, uncurling.
A man!

I am Brook.
This is my dad.

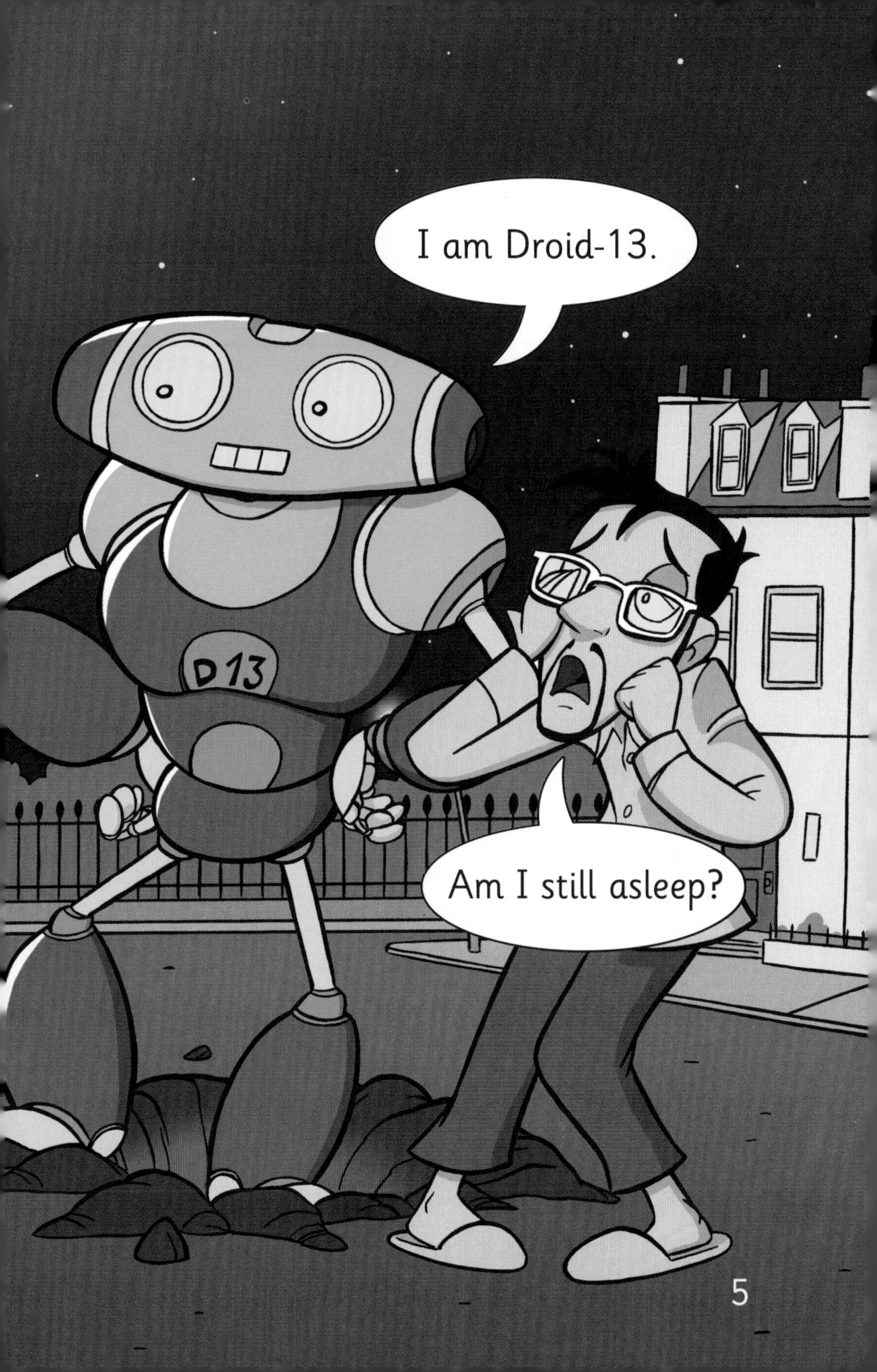
I am Droid-13.
D 13
Am I still asleep?

"I fell from my ship," says Droid-13, pointing up. "I was fixing it."

"A starship?" I frown.

"I must still be asleep, that explains it,"
Dad says, rubbing his brow.

Droid-13 marches to a streetlight.
Clank, clank, clank.

I am shocked. Droid-13 has hands and feet that cling to steel.

You are a magnet man!

Droid-13 yells, "Get back, I cannot keep my grip!"
He crashes down.

"My magnets are not strong, I am frail," complains Droid-13. "My ship will never track me down."

Dad thinks. "I sort steel scrap with a big magnet at the scrapyard," he says.

We bring Droid-13 to Dad's scrapyard.
Droid-13 boosts his magnetic hands and feet
from the magnet.

Droid-13 speeds up a steel hoist. His starship swoops out of the gloom and he shoots into the air.

Dad plods off to bed. I spot a red point of light in the stars, and I grin.

Something odd has melted a pit in the tarmac by this block of flats.

Magnets attract ...

attract

N S

... and repel

repel

Magnets at the scrapyard

Magnet man and me

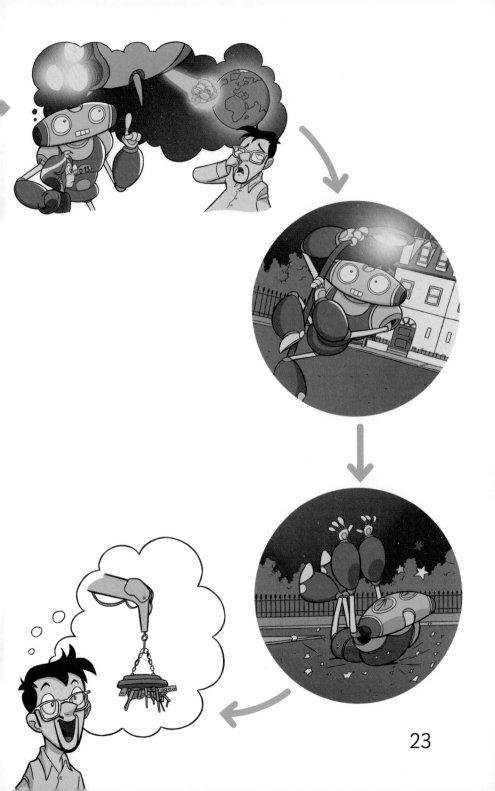

Review: After reading

Use your assessment from hearing the children read to choose any GPCs, words or tricky words that need additional practice.

Read 1: Decoding

- Write **point** on the board and ask the children what it means. (e.g. *sharp corner, tip, place, spot; indicate with a finger*). Then point to the word on page 15. Ask: What does it mean here? (e.g. *place, spot*)
- Encourage the children to practise reading words that contain adjacent consonants with long vowels.
  - o Turn to page 11 and point to **complains**. Ask your child to sound out and blend. (*c/o/m/p/l/a/i/n/s*)
  - o Repeat for: page 12 **steel** (*s/t/ee/l*); page 13 **boosts** (*b/oo/s/t/s*); page 14 **hoist** (*h/oi/s/t*)
- Challenge the children to read the speech bubbles on page 17 fluently. Say: Can you blend in your head when you read the words?

Read 2: Prosody

- Model reading page 6, using different and expressive voices for the characters. Discuss your reading, including how you tried to make Brook sound curious.
- Turn to page 7 and discuss how Dad might sound. Ask: How do you think he's feeling? (e.g. *tired and relieved*)
- Ask children to take turns to read the parts of Droid-13, Brook and Dad expressively while you read the narrative.

Read 3: Comprehension

- Ask the children if they have read any other stories about beings who have arrived in spaceships. Encourage them to explain what the being was like, and what made them unusual.
- Focus on the name **Droid-13** on page 5. Ask the children what **Droid** might be short for. (*android*) If necessary explain what an android is (*a robot that looks slightly human*). Ask: Does that fit the way Magnet Man looks?
- Challenge the children to retell the story using the pictures on pages 22 and 23 as prompts. Suggest they tell it from Brook's viewpoint, starting with "I looked out my bedroom window and saw …".
- Turn to pages 20 and 21 and encourage the children to guess what is happening at each stage of the cycle. Challenge them to use the following vocabulary in their descriptions:
  magnet   **attract**   **sparks**   **steel**
- Bonus content: Look together at pages 18 and 19, and ask the children to describe the key aspects of a magnet. Can they use the images to describe ways in which a magnet can attract and repel?